THE
SECRET
POWER
OF
366
PRAYER & GOODWILL
TEXT MESSAGES

ACKNOWLEDGMENT

I thank the Lord God Almighty for the grace, mercy and inspiration that has made the inception and writing of this book possible. Truly, nothing is impossible.

I dedicate this book to God the father, God the son and to God the Holy Spirit. I also dedicate this book to this Lordship; Bishop Ralph Ebirien, Bishop of the Niger Delta Diocese and to my family; Lady Juliet Andrew-Jaja, Asigha Andrew-Jaja, Henry and Eden Witte and Sokari Andrew-Jaja II.

My appreciation goes to Firstcam Creative Studios for the design and assiduous input in the printing of this book.

PREFACE

One of the ways to get what you want is to send prayer and goodwill text messages to the person from whom you want favor. Do you want a job, contract, promotion or elevation in your venture? Is someone responsible for these favors you want?

Everybody appreciates prayers and being prayed for, and that includes you. Everybody appreciates those who genuinely wish them well and that includes you.

I am strongly recommending you send prayers and goodwill text messages every day to persons you expect to assist you. Initially the person may not consider your request but I assure you if you consistently and persistently send prayer and goodwill text messages, your request will be granted.

Read the parable of the persistent widow. Luke 18:1-5.
"Then He spoke a parable to them, that men always ought to pray and not lose heart, saying:
"There was in a certain city a judge who did not fear God nor regard man. Now there was a widow in that city; and she came to him saying, 'Get justice for me from my adversary.' And he would not for a while; but afterwards he said to himself, 'Though I do not fear God nor regard man, yet because this widow troubles

*me I will avenge her, lest by her continual coming she
weary me.'"*

INTRODUCTION

Do you want that job?
Do you want that contract?
Do you want that promotion?
Do you want that elevation?
Do you want to keep that marriage?
Do you want to get whatever you want?
Do you want to be a winner all the time?
All these are possible.

Here is a secret. That which is a repository of a thing does not lack that thing. A sea gives water and cannot lack water in itself. Air gives breath and cannot in itself lack air. From the days of the Tower of Babel (Genesis 11:3-9) when sand was used to make bricks to build houses, the earth that gives sand has never lacked sand.
In like manner, if you are a repository of blessings and goodwill messages and send same to others, you will never in yourself lack blessings and goodwill.

"Give and it will be given to you: good measure, pressed down, shaken together, and running over will be put into your bosom. For with the same measure that you use, it will be measured back to you." -Luke 6:38. NKJV.

That is the secret. Try it. It works!

Here are 366 blessings and goodwill messages, one for each day of the year, quoted, interpreted and culled straight from the Holy Bible to send each day to your spiritual leader, your boss, your spouse, your mentor, your colleagues, your business associates and partners. Send to even your enemies and haters (Matthew 5:44).

I assure you that in no time at all you will achieve success, wealth, good health, prosperity and abundance. Try it. It works.

THE SECRET POWER OF PRAYER AND GOODWILL TEXT MESSAGES.

DAY 1

God said, "Let there be light", and there was light. Gen. 1:3. May the light of God continue to shine on you always.

DAY 2

The Lord shall meet you with blessings of goodness. He shall set a crown of pure gold upon your head. Psalms 21:3

DAY 3

God shall give you life, length of days, forever and ever. His glory is great in your salvation. Psalm 21.

DAY 4

He shall place upon you, honor and majesty. He shall make you His most blessed forever. He shall make you exceedingly glad in His presence. Psalm 21.

DAY 5

You are part of God's plan. His plan is to abundantly supply all your needs. You shall rise and shine because the spirit of God is in you. Nobody can stop God's plans for you.

God has manifested His miracle in you, through His Son,
JESUS CHRIST

DAY 6

Those who seek to destroy your soul, shall be ashamed and confused. Those that wish you evil shall be desolate and driven backwards. The Lord's truth and loving-kindness shall continually preserve you. Psalm 40:14-15.

DAY 7

God shall protect and prosper you. You shall be a virtuous lady of nations. Your sons shall become kings. Women shall call you "Blessed". Your enemies shall become your foot mat in Jesus' Name. Amen.

DAY 8

God of mercy, God of grace, show the brightness of Your face, shine upon you Savior shine. Fill you with light divine and extend your health and wealth. –A&M 264.

DAY 9

This month, the Lord will keep and sustain you like Noah, favor you like Mary, fight for you like David, anoint you like Deborah and bless you like Abraham.

DAY 10

O God! The author of peace and the lover of concord, in knowledge of whom stands our eternal life, whose service is perfect freedom, defend your humble servant in all assault of the enemy, that surely trusting in your defense, shall not fear the power of any adversaries through the might of JESUS CHRIST mercies.

DAY 11

New day, new life, new mercy, new grace, new hope, new strength, new peace, new joy, new song, new breakthrough, God has made all things new from now on. –Lamentation 3:22-26.

DAY 12

God will give you whatever you ask. With God, all things are possible. On Mount Zion there shall be deliverance and there shall be holiness. Your house shall possess its possessions. –Obadiah 1:17.

DAY 13

This is the first days, the day of light, peace, rest and prayer. Your gloomy nights, troubled mind, waves of strife are gone. God has come to meet you at your point of need. Amen.

DAY14

Arise and shine, your light has come. The glory of God is upon you. He has scattered your enemies and they shall bow. The Lord of Host is with you, the God of Jacob is your refuge.

DAY 15

God is your strength. Your enemies will stumble and fall as God continues to bless you.

DAY 16

You shall be a royal crown of glory in the hand of God. You shall no more be called "forsakcn", neither shall your family be called "barren". But you will be called "Hephzibah" and your land called "Beulah". God is happy with you and your family shall prosper. Rise and Shine.

DAY 17

Morning by morning you see new mercies. God's Hands has provided all you need. Great is God's faithfulness to you. You have been ordained Captain of men and to take our community to the next level. Rise and Shine. God is your strength and shield.

DAY 18

Almighty God shall keep you from falling. His countenance, grace and mercies shall always shine upon you. He will hide you in His Holy tabernacle to protect, prosper and grant you wisdom. He has anointed your head with oil and made you captain of your family. His Holy mantle shall always cover you in the mighty holy name of Jesus Christ.

DAY 19

May God grant you good, sweet night rest. May the Almighty keep you and send His angels round your house to protect you and your family from evil. God has decreed that you should wake up in good health, prosperity and success in your business and long life in the Holy Name of Jesus. Amen.

DAY 20

God said, "I will open a well where there is no well. I will open a way, where there is no way. I have heard your cry, I will open the gates of heaven and I will flood you with blessings, glory, abundant wealth and long life." Amen.

DAY 21

God's blessed assurance is that you will prosper, progress more and stay healthy. You will remain safer under the shadow of the Almighty. You shall not die. Lo, He is with you always.

DAY 22

Almighty God who has brought you this far, shall continue to protect, prosper and bless, you and your family. He shall continue to make right your path.

DAY 23

You are like Mount Zion which cannot be moved. As the mountains surround Jerusalem, so God's countenance, mercy and grace surround you now and always.

DAY 24

You are too blessed to be cursed, too exalted to be humbled, too anointed to be disappointed, too rich to be poor, too protected to be destroyed, too holy to be defiled. You are special in God's Kingdom.

DAY 25

It was not the nails that kept Jesus on the Cross, but His love for you.

DAY 26

Hidden in that Cross is an amazing love that is so divine, survey it, experience it, breath it, embrace it and share it as we live by the grace of God.

DAY 27

You are specially blessed now and always in Jesus Name.

DAY 28

I wish you a new morning with new happiness. May the glory of God overwhelm you in all your undertakings on this beautiful day that the Lord has made. You are blessed.

DAY 29

God has safely brought you from sleep and darkness, restored in you, life, power and thought. This is proof of His new every morning love to you. He will keep you free from harm, in all you say and do today.

DAY 30

Rejoice in the Lord. God is your hiding place. God shall save you from trouble and surround you with songs of deliverance. Arise! God has appeared to you.

DAY 31

God will keep His covenant with you. Your harvest will be plentiful. God will live with you. He will never turn away from you. He will let you walk with your head held high. Leviticus 26:9-13.

DAY 32

God will give you peace in your land. You will sleep without being afraid of anyone. He will rid your land of dangerous animals. You will be victorious over your enemies. 5 of you will defeat a 100 and your 100 will defeat 10,000. Leviticus 26:6-8.

DAY 33

You will still be harvesting corn when it is time to pick grapes. You will still be picking grapes when it is time to sow corn. You will have all you want to eat and live in safety in your land. Leviticus 26:4-5.

DAY 34

God has given you authority to walk on snakes and scorpions, overcome all power of the enemy and nothing will hurt you. Luke 10:19.

DAY 35

The peace of God which passes all understanding, shall keep
your heart and mind through Christ Jesus.
Philippians 4:7.

DAY 36

God has chosen you and separated you from the masses. He has
set you among kings and princes. He has given you the
dynamic ability to change things. You are indeed an
instrument of true value.

DAY 37

As you rise today, God's favor will locate you, His grace will
be with you, His mercy will shine on you and His angels
will be your guide. You are highly favored.

DAY 38

Then you were distinguished above the Judges, Magistrates and
Registrars, because you have an excellent spirit. And the
king thought to set you over the whole realm. Daniel 6:3.

DAY 39

"Peace is what I leave with you. It is my own peace that I give
to you. I do not give it as the world does. Do not be worried
and upset, do not be afraid." John 14:27.

DAY 40

You are together with Jesus in the holy heavenly realm. The life of God is in you. You have dominion over sin and sicknesses, and above all, over principalities and powers.

DAY 41

The spirit of excellence is in you. God has separated you from mediocrity and failure. He has set you apart for the life of excellence and success.

DAY 42

God has given you wisdom and sound mind to function excellently in all you do, in Jesus' Name. Amen.

DAY 43

In stormy, dark times, His oath, covenant, blood and unchanging grace will support you.

DAY 44

Jesus is the solid rock on which you stand. Your future is secured and sanctified. Amen.

DAY 45

God's peace, prosperity and progress reigns supreme in you.

May the hearts of those around you be ignited with true loyalty and dedication to you. You are born to win, in the Name of Jesus. Amen.

DAY 46

You are God's dwelling place. God moves and talks through you. You convey eternal verity and divine nature. You effect positive changes around you because the Greater One lives in you.

DAY 47

God forbids your feet to stumble. God forbids you and your family to hunger and thirst. God forbids the minds and eyes of evil around you. God forbids what you forbid.

DAY 48

May bounteous God, through all your life be near you. Cheer you with joyful heart and blessed peace. Keep you in His grace, guide you when perplexed and free you from all ills. A&M 379.

DAY 49

God will save you from the snares of hell. Goodness and mercy shall follow you, all your days.

DAY 50

God clothes the flowers, feeds the birds. Would He pay you less attention? Look up to God with prayerful heart, He will supply all your needs.

DAY 51

"Remember that I have commanded you to be determined and confident. Do not be afraid or discouraged, for I, the Lord your God, am with you wherever you go." Joshua 1:9.

DAY 52

Today, God has reaffirmed His eternal covenant with you, that He will never abandon you. He will be your helper and provide all good things you need through Jesus Christ.

DAY 53

Now that daylight fills the sky, the Lord will keep you from harm. He will hide you from strife and keep your conscience pure. The Lord shall bless you for all time in the Name of Jesus.

DAY 54

Praise God that will always keep you from falling. His countenance shall always shine on you. You will never lack anything of value. He will satisfy you with long life.

DAY 55

"For God has not given you the spirit of fear, but of power, love and sound mind." 2Timothy 1:7.

DAY 56

God has emboldened, strengthened and fortified you to do your calling. Feelings of timidity, shyness and intimidation are not your portion in Jesus' Name.

DAY 57

You were there when God placed the clouds in the sky, opened the springs of the ocean and ordered the waters of the sea to rise. You were there when He laid the earth's foundation. You are God's daily source of joy.

DAY 58

God has blessed you spiritually in heavenly places. Nothing can stop your progress and success. You live in the kingdom of light where God is your defender and provider.

DAY 59

You are wisdom, understanding and God's image. You were born before the mountains, before the hills were set in place, before God made the earth and its fields or even the first handful of soil. Proverbs 8:25-26

DAY 60

You are wisdom, understanding and God's image. You were there when He set the sky in place, when He stretched the horizon across the ocean. Proverbs 8:27.

DAY 61

You are wisdom, understanding and God's image. The lord created you first, the first of His works long ago. You were made in the very beginning, before the world began. You were born before the oceans. Proverbs 8:22-24.

DAY 62

God will deliver and keep you safe from hidden faults. You will be perfect and free from the evil of sin. Rise and shine.

DAY 63

May the words of your mouth and the meditations of your heart, be acceptable to God your refuge and redeemer. Psalm 19.

DAY 64

There is no mountain too high, no valley nor sea too deep, no vision, dream or goal too big for you to achieve your destiny.

DAY 65

You are a believer with a prevailing faith that works. With God, all things are possible unto you.

DAY 66

The holy spirit in you is the same when David met the lion, bear and Goliath. It is the same holy spirit in Samson, Moses, Joshua and Elijah. You have taken advantage of the holy spirit in you to bless your world.

DAY 67

"You have not chosen me, I have chosen and ordained you…whatsoever you ask of the Father in my Name, He will give it to you. John 15:16.

DAY 68

Your patience and diligence has brought you a life of success, progress, peace and prosperity. God's presence in your life makes you great. He has given you life more abundantly.

DAY 69

Your help comes from the Lord, He will not let you fall. Your protector is always awake. The sun and moon will not hurt you. Psalm 121.

DAY 70

The Lord is by your side, to keep you safe from all danger. He will protect you as you come and go, now and always. Psalm 121.

DAY 71

Your path is a light that shines brighter unto a perfect day. Proverb 4:18.

DAY 72

God has ordained you to be fruitful and productive. You produce success and permanent prosperity.

DAY 73

You are pure and innocent in heart. You see the positive side of things around you. You are counted among the great and faithful.

DAY 74

Your life is the good news of the salvation and ingenuity of Jesus Christ. Shine on!

DAY 75

The divine energy of God is in you. Nothing is impossible for you to accomplish because of the anointing that is working in you through His Son Jesus Christ.

DAY 76

Christ is your peace. He has reconciled you to God in one body by the Cross. You are the body and spirit of Christ. The peace of God be with you.

DAY 77

Do not doubt God's willingness to answer you speedily when you pray. Ask God, He will grant you the desires of your heart.

DAY 78

God said, "I will make my home and live among you. I will be your God and you will be mine. I will accept you and be your Father." You are the temple of the living God.

DAY 79

God has secured your destiny. He has made you a minister of reconciliation. He has put you in the path of success and greatness.

DAY 80

May the Lord your God take great delight in you. He shall continue to protect you in the hollow of His Hands and under the shadows of His wings.

DAY 81

May the heavenly hosts rejoice over you as God's blessed assurance is that you will prosper, progress and stay healthy.

DAY 82

You will remain safe under the shadows of the Almighty God. You shall not die. Lo, He is with you always.

DAY 83

God has given you protection, prosperity and excellent health. Desire it, believe it and claim it.

DAY 84

Almighty God who has brought you this far, shall continue to keep and bless you. He has decreed that you must live to see next year.

DAY 85

God shall continue to make right, your words and deeds. His mantle of grace shall continue to exalt, protect and prosper you.

DAY 86

Almighty God has promised you will be strong as the Iroko. You shall feel the radiance and glory of God. In health and wealth, He shall put you above others.

DAY 87

His banner of love, His pillar of fire are around you. Your enemies will run and scatter in frustration and defeat.

DAY 88

God has crowned you in Zion. He has blessed you. God's covenant with you is that you shall prosper and live. You shall not die young. Jesus will always be your redeemer.

DAY 89

You will forever be God's favorite. Heaven will forever take delight in you. God's grace will cause men to favor you and you will never labor for what is yours.

DAY 90

God is with you. No weapon fashioned against you shall prosper. All evil thoughts and deeds of the devil must return to sender. You have jumped and passed.

DAY 91

Whatever God does, it shall be forever. Nothing can be added to it, and nothing can be taken from it. Ecclesiastes 3:14.

DAY 92

The mountain of the Lord's house, shall be established on the top of the mountains, and shall be exalted above the hills, and people shall flow to it. Micah 4:1.

DAY 93

But everyone shall sit under his vine and under his fig tree, and no one shall make them afraid. For the mouth of the Lord of hosts has spoken. Micah 4:4.

DAY 94

"And it shall come to pass in the last days, says God, that I will pour out My Spirit on all flesh." Acts 2:17.

DAY 95

"…And it shall come to pass that whoever calls on the name of the Lord, shall be saved." Acts 2:21.

DAY 96

"Fill the earth and subdue it. Have dominion over everything that moves on the earth." Genesis 1:28. You are great. You are a conqueror.

DAY 97

"You are gods" John 10:34. The scriptures acknowledge that you interface and partner with God. You are God's image on earth.

DAY 98

"But now in Christ Jesus you… have been brought near by the blood of Christ." Eph. 2:13. You are near to Christ Jesus and no evil shall come near you.

DAY 99

You belong to a chosen generation that has obtained God's mercy. -1 Peter 2:9.

DAY 100

God shall establish His covenant with you and all your family, your loved ones and you shall enter into God's peace and safety. Gen. 6:18.

DAY 101

"In returning and rest you shall be saved. In quietness and confidence shall be your strength." Is. 30:15.

DAY 102

The Lord will wait the He may be gracious to you. The Lord will be exalted that He may have mercy on you. -Is. 30:18.

DAY 103

The Lord will wait that He may be gracious to you. The Lord will be exalted that He may have mercy on you. -Is. 30:18.7. The everlasting God, the Lord, gives you power and increases your strength. Is. 40:28-29.

DAY 104

The everlasting God, the Lord, gives you power and increases your strength. Is. 40:28-29.

DAY 105

God shall renew your strength and you shall mount up with
wings like an eagle. You shall run and not be weary and
walk and not be faint. Is. 40:31.

DAY 106

God is shining into your heart the light of knowledge of the
glory of God in the face of Jesus Christ. II Corinthians 4:6.

DAY 107

You are hard-pressed on every side, yet not crushed. You are
perplexed, but not in despair. You are persecuted, but not
forsaken. You are struck down but not destroyed. II
Corinthians 4:8-9.

DAY 108

God's grace is sufficient for you. His strength is made perfect in
your weakness. You are strong. II Corinthians 12:9.

DAY 109

In the 10th month, on the 1st day of the month, the tops of the
mountains were seen. Gen. 8:5. So shall all see your
intelligence, hard work, integrity and strong character.

DAY 110

"While the earth remains seedtime and harvest, cold and heat, winter and summer, day and night shall not cease." Gen. 8:22. Our relationship shall not cease. Your kindness shall not cease.

DAY111

Surely goodness and mercy shall follow you all the days of your life, and you will dwell in the house of the Lord forever. Ps. 23:6.

DAY 112

I will make you a great nation. I will bless you and make your name great and you shall be a blessing. I will bless those who bless you and curse those who curse you. In you all the families of the earth shall be blessed. Gen. 12:2-3.

DAY 113

Lift up your eyes now and look from the place where you are; northwards, southwards, eastwards and westwards for all the prosperity, wealth, abundance, grace and mercy which you see, God has given to you and your descendants forever. Gen. 13:14-15.

DAY 114

God the Possessor of heaven and earth has delivered your enemies into your hands. Gen. 14:19-20

DAY 115

Do not be afraid, God is your shield, your exceedingly great reward. Gen. 15:1.

DAY 116

God shall multiply your descendants exceedingly that they shall be more than multitude. Gen. 16:10.

DAY 117

God has established His covenant between Him and you and your descendants to bless, protect and prosper you. Gen 17:7.

DAY 118

Is anything too hard for the Lord? At the appointed time, God shall return to you according to the time of life. Gen. 18:14.

DAY 119

God has redeemed your life from destruction and crowned you with loving kindness and tender mercies. Psalms 103:4.

DAY 120

God has satisfied your mouth with good things and your youth is renewed like the eagle's. Psalm 103:5.

DAY 121

As the heavens are high above the earth, so is the height of
DAY 121

As the heavens are high above the earth, so is the height of God's mercy towards you. Psalms 103:11.

DAY 122

You are called according to God's purpose, for you, all things work together for good. Romans 8:28.

DAY 123

God is your rock, fortress and deliverer. He is the God of your strength, your shield and the horn of your salvation. He is your stronghold, refuge and salvation, who saves you from violence. II Samuel 22:2-3.

DAY 124

God drew you out of many waters and has delivered you from your strong enemy and from those who hate you. II Samuel 22:17-18.

DAY 125

God is your support. He has brought you out into a broad place
and delivered you because He delights in you. II Samuel
22:19-20.

DAY 126

God has rewarded you according to your righteousness and the
cleanness of your hands. II Samuel 22:21.

DAY 127

You are merciful, God will show you mercy. You are
blameless,
God has shown you blameless. You are pure, God has shown
you purity. II Samuel 22:26.

DAY 128

God is your lamp. He has lighted up all around you, and you
can run against a troop and leap over a wall. II Samuel
22:29-30.

DAY 129

God is your shield, strength and power. He makes your way
perfect, makes your feet like the feet of a deer and sets you
in high places. II Samuel 22:31-34.

DAY 130

God's gentleness has made you great. He has enlarged the path under you so your feet did not slip. II Samuel 22:36-37.

DAY 131

You have pursued your enemies and did not turn back till they were wounded and destroyed and fallen under your feet. II Samuel 22:38-39.

DAY 132

"In returning and rest you shall be saved. In quietness and confidence shall be your strength." Isaiah 30:15.

DAY 133

God shall grant you according to the riches of His glory. You shall be strengthened with might through His spirit inside you. Ephesians 3:16.

DAY 134

Christ and the fullness of God live in you and you know the width, length, depth and height of Love. Ephesians 3:17-19.

DAY 135

God found you and nurtured you with honey, oil, lambs, goats and wheat. He has kept you as the apple of His Eyes. Deuteronomy 32:10-14.

DAY 136

You are like a tree planted by the waters. You do not fear when heat comes and your leaves are always green. Jeremiah 17:78.

DAY 137

You have authority to trample on snakes and scorpions and to overcome all the power of the enemy, nothing will harm you. Luke 10:19.

DAY 138

God shall prolong your days and the pleasure of the Lord shall prosper in your hands. Isaiah 53:10.

DAY 139

God has raised you to show His power in you. Romans 9:17. God will send a blessing that will overwhelm you.

DAY 140

You are like a tree planted by the waters. You bear fruits in season. Your leaves do not wither and whatsoever you do shall prosper. Psalms 1:3.

DAY 141

You can do all things through Christ who strengthens you. Philippians 4:13.

DAY 142

God shall supply shall you needs according to His riches in glory. Philippians 4:19.

DAY 143

God has given you sufficiency through the new covenant of the Spirit that gives life. II Corinthians 3:5-6.

DAY 144

The Lord is your light and salvation. The Lord is the strength of your life and you shall not be afraid of anyone. Psalms 27:1.

DAY 145

God has granted you wisdom, knowledge, riches, wealth, and honor such that no one before or after you shall have. II Chronicles 1:11-12.

DAY 146

The love of God is poured out in your heart by the Holy Spirit.
Romans 5:5.

DAY 147

You are the blessed pure in heart. You shall see God. Matthew
5:8.

DAY 148

You are not under law. You are under the grace of God and
sins shall not have dominion over you. Romans 6:14.

DAY 149

You have clean hands and a pure heart. You ascend to the hill
of the Lord and stand in His holy place and receive
blessings from the Lord. Romans 24:3-5.

DAY150

In the name of Jesus Christ, you shall cast out demons and you
shall speak with a new tongue. Mark 16-17.

DAY 151

If you pick up snakes and drink anything deadly, it shall not
harm you. You shall lay hands on the sick and they will
recover. Mark 16:18.

DAY 152

"Grace to you and peace from God our Father and the Lord Jesus Christ." Ephesians 1:2.

DAY 153

God has adopted you as His son according to the good pleasure of His will, to the praise and glory of His grace. Ephesians 1:5-6.

DAY 154

God has chosen and blessed you with every spiritual blessing in the heavenly places. Ephesians 1:3.

DAY 155

You are the heir of God and joint-heir with Christ and therefore glorified together. Romans 8:17.

DAY 156

God has called you by glory and virtue and His divine power has given you all things that concerns life and godliness. II Peter 1:3.

DAY 157

All things present, all things to come, all are yours. I Corinthians 3:21-22.

DAY 158

God has made all grace abound toward you that you always have all things sufficiently and abundantly. II Corinthians 9:8.

DAY 159

Your faith has produced, promoted, appreciated and understood the precise knowledge of every good thing in Christ Jesus. Philemon 1:6.

DAY 160

God has granted you favor in the sight of people. Therefore, what you request shall be granted. Exodus 12:36.

DAY 161

You have planted and given bountifully. You shall therefore reap and be given bountifully. II Corinthians 9:6.

DAY 162

God has made you rich for your sake and through the grace of our Lord Jesus Christ. II Corinthians 8:9

DAY 163

God has put within you a new heart and a new spirit and you shall never lack anything of value. Ezekiel 36:26-30.

DAY 164

Though you walk through the valley of the shadow of death, you shall not fear, for God is with you to comfort you. Psalms 23:4.

DAY 165

God has anointed your head with oil and has given you prosperity and good health in abundance right in the presence of your enemies. Psalms 23:5.

DAY 166

Surely goodness and mercy shall follow you and you shall live in God's presence all the days of your life and forever. Psalms 23:6.

DAY 167

God has given you a gift that by grace and faith, you are saved. Ephesians 2:8.

DAY 168

You are a winner. You have wrestled against principalities, powers, rulers of the darkness of this world, against spiritual wickedness in high places and won. Ephesians 6:12.

DAY 169

Lift up your eyes and see. Your help comes from the Lord who made heaven and earth. Psalms 121:1-2.

DAY 170

You have pity and give to the poor. You are giving loan to the Lord. The Lord shall pay back what you have given. Proverbs 19:17.

DAY 171

Rejoice greatly. Do not sorrow. The joy of the Lord is your strength. Nehemiah 8:10-12.

DAY 172

God shall bless you and be merciful to you. He shall cause His face to shine upon you. Psalms 67:1.

DAY 173

Lo! A voice from heaven saying concerning you, "This is my beloved son, whom I am well pleased." Matthew 3:17.

DAY 174

God is on your side, who can be against you? Romans 8:31.

DAY 175

It is God who justifies. You are God's elect. Who is he who condemns? Who shall bring a charge against you? Romans 8:33-34.

DAY 176

In all tribulations, you are more than conqueror through God who loves you. Romans 8:37.

DAY 177

Neither death, life, angels, principalities, powers, things present, things to come, height nor depth shall separate you from the love of God. Romans 8:38-39.

DAY 178

Your tongue does not speak evil and your lips do not lie therefore you shall enjoy life and see many days. 1 Peter 3:10.

DAY 179

You are made in God's image, as you speak, the light of God manifests in you and all darkness disappears.

DAY 180

You are made holy by the holy sacrifice of our Lord, Jesus Christ. John 17:19.

DAY 181

The Lord God Almighty says, He is your Father and you are His son. 2 Corinthians 6:18.

DAY 182

God heard you at the right time. On the day of salvation, He helped you. Today is the day of salvation. 2 Corinthians 6:2.

DAY 183

Rivers of living water is flowing into your heart and you shall never thirst. John 7:37-38.

DAY 184

You are blessed, you delight in the law of the Lord. You do not walk in the counsel of the ungodly nor stand in the path of sinners. Psalm 1:1-2

DAY 185

God has begotten you and shall give you nations for your
inheritance and the ends of the earth for your possession.
Psalms 2:7-8.

DAY 186

The Lord is your shield and glory. He is the One who lifts
up your head and will hear your voice from His Holy
hill. Psalms 3:3-4.

DAY 187

You will sleep and wake and will not be afraid of ten
thousands of people because the Lord sustains you.
Psalms 3:5-6.

DAY 188

Salvation belongs to the Lord and His blessing is upon you.
The Lord has struck down your enemies. He has saved
you. Psalms 3:7-8.

DAY 189

The Lord has heard your prayer and has granted you mercy
and relieved you in distress. Your glory can never turn to
shame. Psalms 4:1-2.

DAY 190

Be still within your heart. The Lord has set you apart for Himself and will hear you whenever you call. Psalms 4:3-4.

DAY 191

The Lord has lifted up the light of His countenance upon you. He makes you dwell in safety and you shall lie down in peace and sleep. Psalms 4:6-8.

DAY 192

The Lord God shall hear your voice and consider your meditation. Psalms 5:1.

DAY 193

You shall come into the house of the Lord in the multitude of His mercy. He shall make His way straight before your face. Psalms 5.

DAY 194

Rejoice and be joyful for you trust in the Lord and he defends you. His favor will surround you like a shield. Psalms 5:11-12.

DAY 195

The Lord shall not rebuke you in His anger nor chasten you in His hot displeasure. He shall have mercy on you and save your soul from trouble. Psalms 6:1-3.

DAY 196

The Lord shall deliver you and save you for His mercies' sake! Evil men shall stay away from you because the Lord has heard your voice. Psalms 6.

DAY 197

The Lord has heard your supplication and has received your prayer. The Lord shall turn back your enemies and put them to trouble and shame. Psalms 6.

DAY 198

Trust God! He shall save and deliver you from those who prosecute you. Your enemies can never tear you like a lion. Psalms 7:1-2.

DAY 199

God shall arise for you to the judgment He has commanded. The Lord shall establish you. He is your defense and savior. Psalms 7.

DAY 200

God will sharpen His sword, bend His bow and make His arrows into fiery shafts for your defense. Psalms 7.

DAY 201

Your enemies have dug out and fallen into the pit which they made. Their trouble and violent dealing shall return upon their heads. Psalms 7:15-16.

DAY 202

God has crowned you with glory and honor. He has made you to have dominion over the works of His Hands and put all things under your feet. Psalms 8:5-6.

DAY 203

God has maintained your right and cause. Your enemies have turned back, fallen and perished in God's presence. Psalms 9:3-4.

DAY 204

God has never forsaken you. He is your refuge in times of trouble. Psalms 9:9-10.

DAY 205

God has lifted you up from the gates of death. He has
considered your troubles and has had mercy on you.
Psalms 9:13.

DAY 206

Your enemies have sunk down in the pit which they made.
Their feet are caught in the net which they hid. Psalms
9:15.

DAY 207

God shall arise! Your enemies are put in fear and turned
into hell. Your expectation shall not perish. Psalms
9:17-20.

DAY 208

Your God does not stand afar off and does not hide in times
of trouble. Psalms 10:1.

DAY 209

God shall arise and set you in safety. He shall preserve you
from this generation forever. Psalms 12:5-7.

DAY 210

God shall never forget you. He shall never hide His face from you and will not allow your enemy to exalt over you. Psalms 13:1-2.

DAY 211

God has enlightened your eyes and you will not sleep the sleep of death. Your enemies and those who trouble you shall not prevail nor rejoice over you. Psalms 13:3-4.

DAY 212

Through His Son; Jesus Christ, God has given you eternal life. 1 John 5:11.

DAY 213

In the fullness of God, you have received grace, glory, wisdom, love, life, strength and wealth. John 1:16.

DAY 214

For as the Father has life in Himself, so has He granted life in the Son and in you. John 5:26.

DAY 215

Through faith you were raised and you are complete in the presence of God. Colossians 2:10.

DAY 216

Love and boldness has been perfected in you. The Lord has made you in His own image. 1 John 4:17.

DAY 217

You are the temple of God and the Spirit of God lives in you. God shall destroy anyone who tries to defile the temple of God which is in you. 1 Corinthians 3:16-17.

DAY 218

You are filled with the knowledge, wisdom and spiritual understanding of the will of God. Colossians 1:9.

DAY 219

By your faith, you move mountains and do great things and nothing is impossible for you to do. Matthew 17:20.

DAY 220

You are God's creation and God in you is greater than anything in this world. 1 John 4:4.

DAY 221

God's word is spirit and the spirit has given you life. Life in abundance. John 6:63.

DAY 222

You are the chosen one. You are God's own royal and holy special person and you are surrounded by His marvelous light. 1 Peter 2:9.

DAY 229

God is the portion of your inheritance and your cup. He has maintained your lot and the lines have fallen to you in pleasant places. Psalms 16:5-6.

DAY 230

God is at your right hand and you shall not be moved. Your heart is glad, your glory rejoices and your flesh will rest in hope. Psalms 16:8-9.

DAY 231

God has shown you the path of life and brought you to fulness of joy and pleasures in His presence. Psalms 16:11.

DAY 232

The Lord has heard your plea for justice. He has paid attention to your prayer and has declared you innocent. Psalms 17:1-2.

DAY 233

God has scrutinized you, tested your thoughts, examined your heart and found nothing wrong. Psalms 17:3

DAY 234

Your steps have stayed on God's path and you have not wavered from following God. Psalms 17:5.

DAY 235

God shows you unfailing love in wonderful ways. By His mighty power He rescues, guards and hides you in the shadow of His Wings. Psalms 17:7-8.

DAY 236

God will guard you as He will guard His own Eyes. He shall protect you from wicked people and murderous enemies. Psalms 17:8-9.

DAY 237

God shall arise and stand against your enemies and bring them to their knees. He shall rescue you with His sword. Psalms 17:13.

DAY 238

God is your strength, rock, fortress, savior and shield. He is your place of safety. Psalms 18:2.

DAY 239

God has heard you from His sanctuary, the ropes of death shall not entangle you. The floods of destruction shall not sweep over you. Psalms 18:4-6.

DAY 240

God reached down from heaven and rescued you from powerful enemies and drew you out of deep waters. Psalms 18:16-17.

DAY 241

The Lord is your shepherd who leads you in watered, green pastures and you shall never lack anything of value. Psalm 23:1-2.

DAY 242

God will generously provide all your needs and you shall have all good things in abundance to share to others. 2 Corinthians 9:8.

DAY 243

God has called you back from the end of the earth. He has chosen you and will not throw you away. Isaiah 41:9.

DAY 244

Do not be afraid. Do not be discouraged. God is with you. He will strengthen you and help you. He will hold you up with His victorious Right Hand. Isaiah 41:10.

DAY 245

"For I know the plans I have for you," says the Lord. "They are plans for good and not for disaster, to give you a future and a hope." Jeremiah 29:11.

DAY 246

God has blessed you. You shall harvest a hundred times more than you sowed. Your abundance in wealth shall continue to grow. Genesis 26:12-13.

DAY 247

Do not fear, there will always be food in abundance in your container. 1 Kings 17:13-14.

DAY 248

Everyone in your family shall eat and there shall even be left over. 2 Kings 4:43.

DAY 249

The laws of the Lord are perfect, trustworthy and right. They revive your soul and bring joy to your heart. Psalms 19:78.

DAY 250

The words of your mouth, the meditations of your heart are acceptable in the sight of God who is your strength and redeemer. Psalm 19:14.

DAY 251

The Lord shall answer you in the day of trouble. The Name of the God of Jacob shall defend you. Psalms 20:1.

DAY 252

God shall send you help from His sanctuary, strengthen you out of Zion and remember your sacrifices. Psalms 20:2-3.

DAY 253

God shall grant you according to your heart's desire and fulfill all your purpose and petitions. Psalms 20:4-5.

DAY 254

You are God's anointed. From His holy heaven, he shall answer and save you with the saving strength of His Right Hand. Psalms 20:6.

DAY 255

The King shall answer you when you call. You have risen and stood upright. Psalms 20:8-9.

DAY 256

Your joy comes from the strength and salvation of God. He has not withheld the request of your lips. Psalm 21:1-2.

DAY 257

God has met you with blessings of goodness. He has set a crown of pure gold upon your head and has given you life. Psalms 21:3-4.

DAY 258

God's glory is great in His salvation. He has placed honor
and majesty upon you and made you most blessed
forever. Psalms 21:5-6.

DAY 259

Your enemies devised a plot they are not able to perform.
The Lord shall swallow up your enemies in His wrath

and fire shall devour them. Psalm 21:9-11.

DAY 260

God shall not forsake you and shall not be far from helping
you. Psalms 22:1.

DAY 261

God shall deliver you from the sword. He shall deliver your
precious life from the power of the dogs. Psalms 22:20.

DAY 262

Your labor has not been in vain in the Lord. You are
steadfast, immovable and abounding in the work of the
Lord. 1 Corinthians 15:58.

DAY 263

The peace of God which surpasses all understanding will
guard your heart and mind through Christ Jesus.
Philippians 4:6.

DAY 264

God has snatched you away from the lion's jaws and from the
horns of wild oxen. Psalms 22:21.

DAY 265

God shall not ignore or belittle you, neither will He turn His
back on you. Psalms 22:24.

DAY 266

Your enemies shall not triumph over you and the Lord shall
not allow you to be put to shame. Psalms 25:2.

DAY 267

The Lord shall show you His ways and teach you His paths.
He shall lead you in His truth because He is the God of
your salvation. Psalms 25:4-5.

DAY 268

The Lord shall remember you according to His mercy and
goodness. He shall continue to guide you in justice.
Psalms 25:7,9.

DAY 269

You shall dwell in prosperity and your descendants shall
inherit the earth. Psalms 25:13.

DAY 270

The secret of the Lord is with you and He shall show you
His covenant. He shall pluck your feet out of the net.
Psalms 25:14-15.

DAY 271

You shall never be desolate nor afflicted nor distressed. The
Lord shall keep your soul and deliver you. Psalms
25:16,17,20.

DAY 272

You walk in integrity and you shall not slip. The Lord has
examined and vindicated you. Psalms 26:1-2.

DAY 273

You walk in God's truth and His lovingkindness is before you. You are in God's altar and your hands are washed in innocence. Psalms 26:3, 6.

DAY 274

God's glory and wondrous works shine all around you. God has redeemed you and your foot stands in an even place. Psalms 26:7, 8, 12.

DAY 275

The Lord is your light and salvation. He is the strength of your life and you shall not be afraid of anyone. Psalms 27:1.

DAY 276

The wicked that came to eat up your flesh and the army that encamped against you, all stumbled and fell. Psalms 27:2-3.

DAY 277

You shall live in the House of the Lord all the days of your life to behold His beauty and inquire in His temple. Psalms 27:4.

DAY 278

God shall hide you in His pavilion and in the secret place of
His tabernacle. God shall set you high upon a rock.
Psalms 27:5.

DAY 279

God has lifted up your head above your enemies as you sing
praises and offer sacrifices of joy in His tabernacle.
Psalms 27:6.

DAY 280

The Lord has heard your voice and has answered and
granted you mercy. Psalms 27:7.

DAY 281

God will not hide His face from you. God shall not turn you
away in anger   nor forsake you. God remains your help
and salvation. Psalms 27:9.

DAY 282

God shall not deliver you to the will of your enemies or
those that breathe out violence. God shall lead you in a
smooth path. Psalms 27:11-12.

DAY 283

Be of good courage. God shall strengthen your heart and you shall see the goodness of the Lord in the land of the living. Psalms 27:13-14.

DAY 284

The Lord is your Rock. He shall not be silent to you and you shall not go down to the pit. Psalms 28:1.

DAY 285

Your hands are lifted towards God's holy sanctuary and He has heard the voice of your supplication. Psalms 28:2.

DAY 286

Your heart rejoices because the Lord is your strength and shield. God has blessed your inheritance and shall bear them up forever. Psalms 28:7-9.

DAY 287

The Lord God shall give you strength and bless you with peace. Psalms 29:11.

DAY 288

God has lifted you and has not let your enemies rejoice over you. Psalms 30:1.

DAY 289

God has kept you alive. He has brought you up from the grave and shall not let you go down to the pit. Psalms 30:3.

DAY 290

Your joy is for life. God's favor is for life. Weeping may endure for a night, but joy comes in the morning. Psalms 30:5.

DAY 291

In your prosperity, you shall never be moved. God has made your mountain stand strong. Psalms 30:6-7.

DAY 292

God shall deliver you speedily. God is your rock of refuge and a fortress of defense to save you. Psalms 31:2.

DAY 293

God has pulled you out from the net which they secretly laid for you. Your spirit is in the Hands of God. Psalms 31:45.

DAY 294

You are glad and joyful in God's mercy. He has not shut you up into the hands of your enemies, but has set your feet in a wide place. Psalms 31:7-8.

DAY 295

Your life shall not waste away with grief. Your strength shall not fail. You shall not be forgotten like a broken vessel. Psalms 31:10-12.

DAY 296

Your enemies can never conspire to scheme to take away your life. Your times are in the Hands of God. Psalms 31:13, 15.

DAY 297

God shall put the wicked to shame. He shall make them to be silent in their graves and their lying lips shall be put to silence, for your sake. Psalms 31:17-18.

DAY 298

God shall hide you in the secret place of His Presence from the plots of man and from the strife of tongues. Psalms 31:20.

DAY 299

God has shown you His marvelous kindness. He has preserved you and strengthened your heart. Psalms 31:21, 23, 24.

DAY 300

There is no deceit in your spirit. The Lord does not impute you with sin, you are blessed. Psalms 32:2.

DAY 301

God shall surround you with songs of deliverance. The flood of great waters shall not come near you. Psalms 32:6-7.

DAY 302

God has done excellent things in your life with joy you shall draw water from the wells of salvation. Isaiah 12:3, 5.

DAY 303

Everyone can see the reflection of the glorious image of God in you. God is a spirit and has made you more and more like Him. 2 Corinthians 3:18.

DAY 304

God who is rich in mercy has exalted you to sit together with Jesus Christ in heavenly places. Ephesians 2:4-6.

DAY 305

God has showered you with His gifts of grace and kindness. Ephesians 2:7-8.

DAY 306

By God's authority you have received power and the Holy Spirit is upon you. Acts 1:8.

DAY 307

Your wisdom has given you the spirit of patience and your favor is like dew on the grass. Proverbs 19:11-12.

DAY 308

We are all confident that God hears you when you ask anything according to His will. 1 John 5:14.

DAY 309

The eyes of the Lord are upon you and His ears are open to your prayers. Who is he that can harm you? 1 Peter 3:1213.

DAY 310

Do not fear. It is God's good pleasure to give you the
kingdom. You have provided for yourself money bags
and treasures in heaven. Luke 12:32-34.

DAY 311

God shall supply all your needs according to His riches in
glory by Christ Jesus. Philippians 4:19.

DAY 312

God is your sun and shield. God has given you grace and
glory and will not withhold any good thing from you.
Psalms 84:11.

DAY 313

The God of peace is with you. You do the things you have
learned, received and heard from God. Philippians 4:9.

DAY 314

God has instructed and taught you in the way you should go.
He has surrounded you with mercy. Be glad and shout for
joy. Psalms 32:8-11.

DAY 315

God has fashioned your heart and blessed you. He has chosen you as His inheritance. Psalms 33:12, 15.

DAY 316

The eyes of the Lord and His mercy are upon you. He has delivered you from death and kept you from any lack. Psalms 33:18-19.

DAY 317

The Lord has heard you and has delivered you from all your fears and shame. He has made you radiant. Psalms 34:4-5.

DAY 318

The Lord has saved you from all your troubles. The angels of the Lord encamp all around you. Psalms 34:6-7.

DAY 319

You have tasted and seen the Lord is good. You are blessed and you do not lack. Psalms 34:8-9.

DAY 320

God has delivered you from all afflictions. He guards your bones and not one is broken. Psalms 34:19-20.

DAY 321

God shall fight those who fight against you. He shall take
up the shield and spear to stop those who pursue you.
Psalms 35:1-3.

DAY 322

God has made you to laugh and your family, friends and all
shall laugh with you. Genesis 21:6.

DAY 323

Arise! Do not fear. God is with you and has made you a
great nation. Genesis 21:17, 18, 20.

DAY 324

"In the Mount of the Lord it shall be provided." God has
blessed you and multiplied your descendants. They shall
possess the gates of your enemies. Genesis 22:14, 17.

DAY 325

"The Lord bless you and keep you. The Lord make His
Face to shine upon you and be gracious to you."
Numbers 6:24-25.

DAY 326

"The Lord lift up His countenance upon you and give you peace." Numbers 6:26.

DAY 327

God is your salvation and those who seek after your life shall be put to shame and dishonor. Psalms 35:3-4.

DAY 328

Those who plot to hurt you shall be turned back and brought to confusion. They shall be like chaff before the wind. Psalms 35:4-5.

DAY 329

The angels of the Lord shall chase your enemies. The path of your enemies shall be dark and slippery. Psalms 35:5-6.

DAY 330

You are a good man and out of the good treasures of your heart, you bring forth good things. Matthew 12:35.

DAY 331

The word of God's grace has built you up and has given you an inheritance among those who are sanctified. Acts 20:32.

DAY 332

The word of Christ dwells in you richly in all wisdom and with grace in your heart. Colossians 3:16.

DAY 333

The Lord God knew you, sanctified you and ordained you long before you were born. Jeremiah 1:5.

DAY 334

God has appeared to you and has delivered and exalted you. Rise and stand on your feet. Acts 26:16-17.

DAY 335

You are a fellow citizen with the saints and member of the household of God. Ephesians 2:19.

DAY 336

The Lord God will give you success and show you kindness. Today, your journey shall be prosperous. Genesis 24:12, 21.

DAY 337

God will bless you and be with you. He has given you and your descendants the land where you dwell. Psalms 26:3.

DAY 338

God began to make you prosper and you continued prospering until you have become prosperous. Genesis 26:13.

DAY 339

Do not fear. God is with you and has blessed you and multiplied your descendants like Abraham. Genesis 26:24.

DAY 340

We have certainly seen that the Lord is with you. You are the blessed of the Lord. Genesis 26:28-29.

DAY 341

God has justified you by your powerful faith. In you all the nations shall be blessed. Galatians 3:8.

DAY 342

The Lord will never forsake you. For His Name's sake, it has pleased Him to make you His own person. 1 Samuel 12:22.

DAY 343

God has led you through the depths and through the
wilderness for His Name's sake, to make His mighty
power known. Psalms 106:8-9.

DAY 344

You serve God in holiness, righteousness and without fear.
God has delivered you from the hand of your enemies.
Luke 1:74-75.

DAY 345

God's kindness shall not depart from you nor shall His
covenant of peace be removed. Isaiah 54:10.

DAY 346

God will lay your stones with colorful gems, your
foundations with sapphires, your pinnacles of rubies,
your gates of crystals and your wall of precious stones.
Isaiah 54:11-12.

DAY 347

You are like a tree planted by the water and brings fruit in
season. You shall not wither and whatever you do shall
prosper. Psalm 1:3

DAY 348

You are my child; I have begotten you. Ask of me and I will give you the nation for your inheritance and the earth for your possession. Blessed are you, who trust in God. Psalm 2:7,8 and 12.

DAY 349

The Lord is your shield. He is your glory and The One that lifts up your head. He hears your voice from His Holy Hill. Psalm 3:3-4.

DAY 350

You will sleep and wake up because the Lord sustains you. You will not be afraid of ten thousand people who have set themselves against you. Psalm 3:5-6.

DAY 351

God shall arise and save you. He has struck your enemies on their cheek bone and broken their teeth. His blessing is upon you. Psalm 3:7-8.

DAY 352

God shall have mercy on you and hear your prayers. He shall relieve you in your distress. The Lord has set you apart for himself. Psalm 4:1,3.

DAY 353

Be still on your bed and meditate within your heart. Offer sacrifices and put your trust in God. Psalm 4:4 and 5.

DAY 354

The Lord will lift up the light of His countenance upon you. He shall put gladness in your heart. Psalm 4:7.

DAY 355

You will sleep in peace because the Lord makes you live in safety. Psalm 4:8.

DAY 356

This morning, God shall hear your prayers, your voice, your cries, your meditation. Psalm 5:1.

DAY 357

You shall come into the house of the Lord, in the multitude of His mercy. Psalm 5:7.

DAY 358

You will rejoice and shout for joy because the Lord defends you and surrounds you with shield of favor. Psalm 5:1112.

DAY 359

The Lord will heal, deliver and show you mercy. He has received your supplication and prayers and put your enemies to shame. Psalm 6.

DAY 360

God shall save and deliver you from your persecutors. They shall not like a lion tear you. Psalm 7:1 and 2.

DAY 361

The wicked will fall into the pit they dug for you. Their trouble and violent dealings which they planned for you shall return upon their head. Psalm 7:15-16.

DAY 362

God is mindful of you and shall visit you. He has crowned you with glory and honor. Psalm 8:4-5.

<h1 style="text-align:center">DAY 363</h1>

God has put you in dominion over the works of His Hands. He has put all things under your feet. Psalm 8:6.

<h1 style="text-align:center">DAY 364</h1>

God has maintained your right and your cause. Your enemies shall turn back and shall fall and perish in God's presence. Psalm 9:3-4.

<h1 style="text-align:center">DAY 365</h1>

God will be your refuge in times of trouble. He shall not forsake you. Psalm 9:9-10.

<h1 style="text-align:center">DAY 366</h1>

God shall consider your trouble from those who hate you. He shall have mercy on you and lift you up from the gates of death. Psalm 9:13.

ABOUT THE AUTHOR

Sir Sokari Dappa Andrew-Jaja; a Knight of,
The Church of Nigeria; Anglican Communion,
is from Opobo in Opobo/Nkoro Local
Government Area of Rivers State of Nigeria.
He attended Big Qua Primary School in Calabar.
He attended Hope Waddell Training Institute in 
Calabar and Mary Knoll College in Okuku, Ogoja. He further attended
the University of Lagos where he obtained a Bachelor of Arts degree in
History and Also attended the Rivers State University; Port-Harcourt
where he obtained the Bachelor of Laws degree. On the 16th of
December, 1992 he was called to the Nigerian Bar by the Body of
Benchers.

He holds a Post-Graduate Diploma Certificate in Petroleum and
Environmental Law.
He was a Special Marshall of the Federal Road Safety Commission,
Port-Harcourt Unit.
He is a Special Patron of the Boys' Brigade of Nigeria.
He is Friend of the Girls' Guide of Nigeria.
He is an Associate of the Alternative Dispute Resolution Institute, 50
Julius Nyerere Crescent in Abuja.
He is conferred with the AWARD OF EXCELLENCE by the
International Federation of Women Lawyers (FIDA).
He is conferred with the AWARD OF EXCELLENCE by the Nigerian
Bar Association Young Lawyers' Forum, Isiokpo Branch.
He is married with children.
He is presently a Chief Magistrate Grade 1 of the Rivers State
Judiciary.